THE WORLD'S WORST NATURAL DISASTERS

THE WORLD'S WORST
FLOODS

by John R. Baker

CAPSTONE PRESS
a capstone imprint

T0052472

Blazers Books are published by Capstone Press,
1710 Roe Crest Drive, North Mankato, Minnesota 56003
www.mycapstone.com

Library of Congress Cataloging-in-Publication Data
Names: Baker, John R. (John Ronald), 1989–
Title: The world's worst floods / by John R. Baker.
Description: North Mankato, Minnesota: Capstone Press, 2017. | Series: Blazers.
  World's worst natural disasters | Includes bibliographical references and index. |
  Description based on print version record and CIP data provided by publisher;
  resource not viewed.
Identifiers: LCCN 2016000444 (print) | LCCN 2015049412 (ebook) | ISBN
  9781515717959 (eBook PDF) | ISBN 9781515717874 (library binding) |
  ISBN 9781515717911 (paperback)
Subjects: LCSH: Floods—History—Juvenile literature.
Classification: LCC GB1399 (print) | LCC GB1399 .B35 2017 (ebook) |
  DDC 551.48/901—dc23
LC record available at http://lccn.loc.gov/2016000444

Summary: Describes history's biggest and most
  destructive floods from around the world.

Editorial Credits
Aaron Sautter, editor; Steve Mead, designer; Jo Miller,
media researcher; Tori Abraham, production specialist

Photo Credits
AP Images: The Southern Illinoisan/Paul Newton, 12–13;
Corbis, 8–9, 20–21, Andrew Holbrooke, 10–11; Gamma-Rapho
via Getty Images: Chip HIRES, 22–23; Getty Images: AFP/
STR, 26–27; iStockphoto: RonBailey, 28–29; Newscom: EPA/
POOL/Vincent Laforet, 14–15, Mondadori/Giorgio Lotti,
16–17, ZUMA Press/KEYSTONE Pictures USA, 24–25; NOAA/
National Weather Service Collection, 18–19; Shutterstock:
leonello calvetti, cover, 3, 31, Lisa S., cover, Vladimir Melnikov,
4–5; The Image Works: Lebrecht, 6–7

Design Elements
Shutterstock: Brisbane, xpixel

TABLE OF CONTENTS

THE POWER OF WATER

A thunderstorm stalls and dumps a massive amount of rain. A huge wall of water sweeps away trees, cars, and homes. Powerful floods bring destruction around the world every year. Find some dry ground. It's time to read about the worst floods in the world.

TYPES OF FLOODS

Floods come in many forms. However they arrive, floods overwhelm land that is normally dry.

FLASH FLOOD:
A stream or river rises quickly and pours over its banks. It's usually caused by heavy rain or a **dam** break.

URBAN FLOOD:
Heavy rain overwhelms city sewers and turns streets into rivers.

REGIONAL FLOOD:
A big river overflows its banks. It covers a large area with water for a long period of time.

ICE JAM FLOOD:
Huge chunks of ice clog a river, causing water to overflow.

STORM SURGE FLOOD:
A hurricane or strong storm pushes seawater inland.

dam—a barrier built to block a body of water

HISTORY'S DEADLIEST FLOOD

Location:
northern China

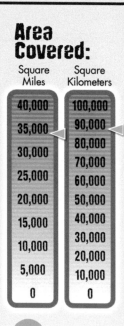

Date:
Summer 1931

Area Covered:

Square Miles	Square Kilometers
40,000	100,000
35,000	90,000
30,000	80,000
	70,000
25,000	60,000
20,000	50,000
15,000	40,000
	30,000
10,000	20,000
5,000	10,000
0	0

During the summer of 1931, heavy rainfall sent China's Huang He River flowing over its banks. The flood covered thousands of square miles. It ruined crops and spread disease. It claimed the lives of about 4 million people.

China's massive 1931 flood left more than 80 million people without homes.

MISSISSIPPI RIVER DISASTER

Location:
Mississippi River Valley

Date:
Spring and summer 1927

Area Covered:

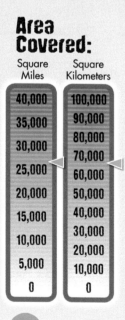

Square Miles	Square Kilometers
40,000	100,000
35,000	90,000
30,000	80,000
	70,000
25,000	60,000
20,000	50,000
15,000	40,000
10,000	30,000
	20,000
5,000	10,000
0	0

Heavy spring rains in 1927 caused the Mississippi River to reach **flood stage**. The water broke **levees** that protected towns and farms. Floodwaters covered millions of acres of land. It damaged 162,000 homes. More than 240 people died.

flood stage—the level a river or stream reaches when it begins to cause damage

levee—a bank of earth or a structure built on the side of a river to keep it from overflowing

GREAT FLOOD OF 1993

Location:
Upper Mississippi River

Date:
Summer 1993

Area Covered:

Square Miles	Square Kilometers
40,000	100,000
35,000	90,000
30,000	80,000
25,000	70,000
	60,000
20,000	50,000
15,000	40,000
10,000	30,000
	20,000
5,000	10,000
0	0

Another major flood occurred along the upper Mississippi River in 1993. It covered 30,000 square miles (78,000 square km) from North Dakota to Missouri. The floodwaters caused $20 billion in damage. It was the costliest flood ever seen in the United States.

MANAGING A MAJOR FLOOD

Location:
Lower Mississippi River

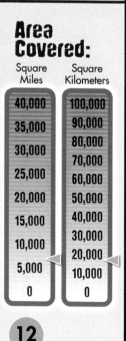

Date:
April to June 2011

Area Covered:

Square Miles	Square Kilometers
40,000	100,000
35,000	90,000
30,000	80,000
	70,000
25,000	60,000
20,000	50,000
15,000	40,000
10,000	30,000
	20,000
5,000	10,000
0	0

In 2011 heavy rains swelled the Ohio and Mississippi Rivers. To save Cairo, Illinois, engineers blew up a levee. This redirected the floodwaters. In Morganza, Louisiana, they opened **spillway** gates. This helped prevent flooding in the city.

In 2011 floodwaters along the lower Mississippi River lasted from April to June. The water reached record levels at Vicksburg and Natchez, Mississippi.

spillway—a structure or passage allowing excess water to move from the main river to another area in order to lower the water level

WHEN THE LEVEES BROKE

Date:
August 29, 2005

Peak Water Height:

Feet	Meters
40	12
35	10
30	8
25	
20	6
15	4
10	
5	2
0	0

Hurricane Katrina roared into New Orleans on August 29, 2005. The storm's 19-foot (5.8-meter) **storm surge** broke through levees. The city was flooded. Thousands of people huddled on roofs and in trees waiting to be rescued.

After the hurricane water covered 80 percent of New Orleans. It was up to 20 feet (6.1 m) deep in some places.

storm surge—a huge wave of water pushed ashore by an approaching hurricane

FLORENCE UNDER WATER

Location:
Florence, Italy

Date:
November 4, 1966

Peak Water Height:

Feet	Meters
40	12
35	10
30	
25	8
20	6
15	4
10	
5	2
0	0

In 1966 three days of heavy rain turned the Arno River into a **torrent**. The water reached up to 10 feet (3 m) high as it raged through Florence, Italy. The flood killed about 100 people. It left 5,000 families homeless.

Florence was famous for its artwork and books. The flood damaged or destroyed millions of rare books and works of art. Some of them were repaired. Others were lost forever.

torrent—a strong, fast-moving stream of water or other liquid

BLACK HILLS FLOOD

Location:
Rapid City, South Dakota

Date:
June 9, 1972

Peak Water Height:

Feet	Meters
40	12
35	10
30	8
25	
20	6
15	4
10	
5	2
0	0

On June 9, 1972, 15 inches (38 centimeters) of rain fell near Rapid City, South Dakota. Rapid Creek became a raging river. Then a nearby dam broke. A flash flood ripped through the city. The flood destroyed 15 bridges. It ruined more than 1,000 homes.

FACT

The Black Hills flood killed 238 people. It did more than $165 million in damage.

DEADLIEST U.S. FLOOD

Location:
Johnstown, Pennsylvania

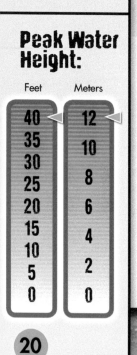

Date:
May 31, 1889

Peak Water Height:

Feet	Meters
40	12
35	10
30	
25	8
20	6
15	4
10	
5	2
0	0

The deadliest flood in U.S. history hit Johnstown, Pennsylvania, on May 31, 1889. Heavy rains and rising water broke a nearby dam. The wall of water ripped apart homes, barns, and bridges. The disaster destroyed about 1,600 homes. It killed 2,209 people.

FACT

Up to 20 million tons
(18.1 million metric
tons) of water rolled
through Johnstown
in the 1889 flood.

BANGLADESH DISASTER

Location:
Bangladesh

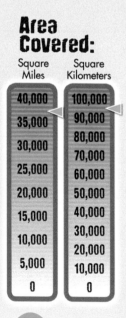

Date:
July to September, 1998

Area Covered:

Square Miles	Square Kilometers
40,000	100,000
35,000	90,000
30,000	80,000
	70,000
25,000	60,000
20,000	50,000
15,000	40,000
10,000	30,000
	20,000
5,000	10,000
0	0

During the summer of 1998, much of Bangladesh was under water. Heavy **monsoon** rains caused severe flooding of the country's main rivers. The water ruined much of the country's food. Wells became dirty. Disease spread quickly.

FACT

The flood in Bangladesh left between 21 and 25 million people homeless.

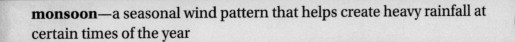

monsoon—a seasonal wind pattern that helps create heavy rainfall at certain times of the year

NORTH SEA TRAGEDY

Location:
Netherlands, Great
Britain, Belgium

Date:
February 1, 1953

Area Covered:

Square Miles	Square Kilometers
40,000	100,000
35,000	90,000
30,000	80,000
	70,000
25,000	60,000
20,000	50,000
15,000	40,000
	30,000
10,000	20,000
5,000	10,000
0	0

tide—the rising and falling of the ocean up and down the shore

Tragedy struck countries around the North Sea on February 1, 1953. A strong storm drove a huge surge of water toward land. Seawater gushed into British villages and farms. Water covered hundreds of square miles in the Netherlands. The flood killed more than 1,800 people. It destroyed 43,000 homes.

FACT

The large storm surge combined with high **tides** to flow over the countries' sea walls and **dikes**.

dike—a strong wall built to keep water from flooding the land

BANQUIAO DAM DISASTER

Location:
China

Date:
August 8, 1975

Peak Water Height:

Feet	Meters
40	12
35	10
30	8
25	
20	6
15	4
10	
5	2
0	0

In 1975 **super-typhoon** Nina dumped more than 40 inches (102 cm) of rain on China. The Banquiao Dam burst on August 8. The wall of water was up to 7 miles (11 km) wide and 33 feet (10 m) high. It wiped out entire villages. Water covered millions of acres of land.

FACT

More than 60 other dams failed in the disaster. The flood destroyed 6 million buildings. It killed 85,600 people. About 140,000 more people later died from disease and a lack of food.

super-typhoon—a large spinning storm in the northwest Pacific Ocean with sustained winds of 150 miles (241 km) per hour or more

STAYING SAFE IN A FLOOD

It's important to know what to do if a flood threatens your area. Try to get to higher ground. Stay away from flooded areas. The water can quickly sweep you off your feet. Floods can be dangerous. Stay safe by keeping calm and knowing what to do.

DISASTER EMERGENCY KIT

An emergency kit can be very helpful in case of a flood. A good kit should include these items:

- ✔ first-aid kit
- ✔ flashlight
- ✔ battery-powered radio
- ✔ extra batteries
- ✔ blankets
- ✔ bottled water
- ✔ canned and dried food
- ✔ can opener
- ✔ whistle to alert rescue workers

dam (DAM)—a barrier built to block a body of water

dike (DYKE)—a strong wall built to keep water from flooding the land

flood stage (FLUD STAYJ)—the level a river or stream reaches when it begins to cause damage

levee (le-VEE)—a bank of earth or a structure built on the side of a river to keep it from overflowing

monsoon (mahn-SOON)—a seasonal wind pattern that helps create heavy rainfall at certain times of the year

spillway (SPIL-way)—a structure or passage allowing excess water to move from the main river to another area in order to lower the water level

storm surge (STORM SURJ)—a huge wave of water pushed ashore by an approaching hurricane

super-typhoon (SOO-pur ty-FOON)—a large spinning storm in the northwest Pacific Ocean with sustained winds of 150 miles (241 km) per hour or more

tide (TYDE)—the rising and falling of the ocean up and down the shore

torrent (TOHR-uhnt)—a strong, fast-moving stream of water or other liquid

READ MORE

Gray-Wilburn, Renée. *Floods: Be Aware and Prepare.* Weather Aware. North Mankato, Minn.: Capstone Press, 2014.

Raum, Elizabeth. *Surviving Floods.* Children's True Stories: Natural Disasters. Chicago: Heinemann-Raintree, 2012.

Richards, Marlee. *The Johnstown Flood: Core Events of a Deadly Disaster.* What Went Wrong? North Mankato, Minn.: Capstone Press, 2014.

INTERNET SITES

Facthound offers a safe, fun way to find Internet sites related to this book. All of the sites on Facthound have been researched by our staff.

Here's all you do:
Visit *www.facthound.com*
Type in this code: 9781515717874

 Check out projects, games and lots more at
www.capstonekids.com

CRITICAL THINKING USING THE COMMON CORE

1. Floods can be deadly and incredibly destructive. How many people died in the deadliest flood ever recorded? Which flood did the most damage in the United States? (Key Ideas and Details)

2. Explain what you should do if a flood threatens your area. (Craft and Structure)

3. Describe the different kinds of floods and how each occur. (Integration of Knowledge and Ideas)

INDEX